Beginners' Programme
to
Plectrum Guitar
(Grade-2)

Beginners' Programme
to
Plectrum Guitar
(Grade-2)

By

Kapil Srivastava

(Guitarmonk)

UNICORN BOOKS

Publishers
UNICORN BOOKS
F-2/16, Ansari Road, Daryaganj, New Delhi-110002
☎ 23275434, 23262683, 23262783 • Fax: 011-23257790
E-mail: info@unicornbooks.in • *Website:* www.unicornbooks.in

Distributors
Pustak Mahal®
J-3/16, Daryaganj, New Delhi-110002
☎ 23276539, 23272783, 23272784 • Fax: 011-23260518
E-mail: info@pustakmahal.com • *Website:* www.pustakmahal.com

Sales Centres

- 10-B, Netaji Subhash Marg, Daryaganj, New Delhi-110002
  ☎ 23268292, 23268293, 23279900 • Fax: 011-23280567
  E-mail: salespmahal@airtelmail.in, rapidexdelhi@indiatimes.com
- 6686, Khari Baoli, Delhi-110006
  ☎ 23944314, 23911979
- Bengaluru: ☎ 080-22234025 • Telefax: 080-22240209
  E-mail: pustak@airtelmail.in • pustak@sancharnet.in
- Mumbai: ☎ 022-22010941, 022-22053387
  E-mail: rapidex@bom5.vsnl.net.in
- Patna: ☎ 0612-3294193 • Telefax: 0612-2302719
  E-mail: rapidexptn@rediffmail.com
- Hyderabad: Telefax: 040-24737290
  E-mail: pustakmahalhyd@yahoo.co.in

ISBN 978-81-7806-223-5

Edition: January, 2011

Printed at : Param Offsetters, Okhla, New Delhi-110020

Preface

I have great pleasure to bring forth this book as part of my endeavour to give some sort of organisation and structure to the music education in India.

Going by my professional experience in the last two decades, I have realized that India badly needs an organized music teaching system. The non-existence of such a system is one of the factors that plagues music education in our country. Non-compulsory music education and lack of awareness are the other factors which add to its present state.

This is the first book of the four volume book series published under the same title. As there is a dearth of constructive content for study and reference on this subject, to a great extent, this book will serve the purpose. The well organized content and the exercises of this book are a first-class study material for the aspiring students of music to prepare for various examinations. Even a 5 year old learner can use this book and it will help him to achieve the desired goal in a short span of time.

It is a matter of great pride and pleasure to note that my other books on music are well received by students and readers alike across the globe. They are also introduced as text books in many schools. We reach out all the places and regions through these books and thus we would be able to serve you without our physical presence.

I thank readers, students and others for their support and patronage. Your suggestions and comments on the further improvement of this book will be thankfully acknowledged and the same will be incorporated in the next edition.

Author

Overview

THE OBJECTIVES

The primary objective of this book is to familiarise the learners with terminologies, exercises and repertoires along with the audios of the compositions. This would help the learners to get a clear perspective on various aspects of the subject.

WHOM IS THIS BOOK FOR?

The book is for complete beginners who know nothing about the instrument, the students who prepare for examinations and the teachers who train the students.

THE SPECIAL FEATURES

- It is customized into levels and can be covered very easily in 12-24 sessions maximum based on time involvement.
- It is an ideal book for teachers who help their student in constructive sessions and productive outcome.
- The book is a step-by-step guide which takes a student from one level to the next. It also inspires success at every grade via achievements which motivates students to get curious and interested in further learning.
- This book contains an audio-CD that instructs on speed and movement of tune: and it is a good reference for the learners who find difficulties in staff reading.
- It contains the basics of staff notations which is very useful information for any music beginner.
- It is a compilation of very significant compositions, rated at a global standard, essential for any music student.

- It offers finger movements which are the most important part for a quality and right learning and support to both teacher and student.
- It offers exercise, pop music repertoire, music theory and Practice Compositions

HOW WILL THIS BOOK HELP YOU?

- It can help you in going about a step-by-step and systematic learning
- A quality and constructive repertoire of songs for your personal performance.
- It instructs you on finger patterns, so as to help both teacher and student with accurate fingering.
- You can expect a basic performance from yourself and can render a medley of tunes on any platform after practicing the given tunes.
- It can assist you, to a great extent, for a performance preparation and content and, thus, it can bring out a musician in you.

Content

EXERCISES

TECHNICAL DEVELOPMENT

(An essential practice for every music student)

Exercise - 11

Left Hand Exercises

(4 Fingers Warm Up)

Moderate ♩ = 180

Going Back...

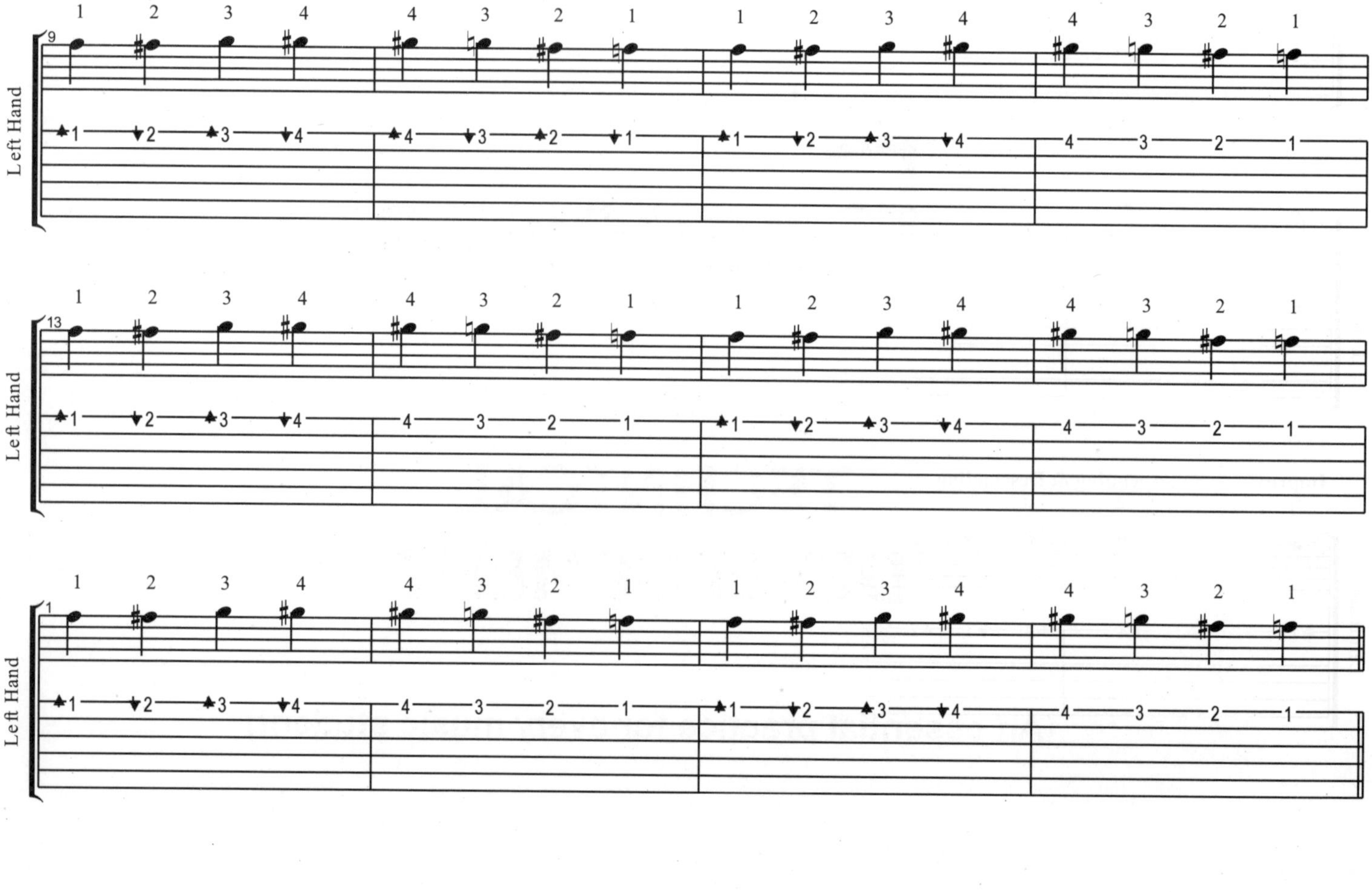

Moving to next frets (1 2 3 4)

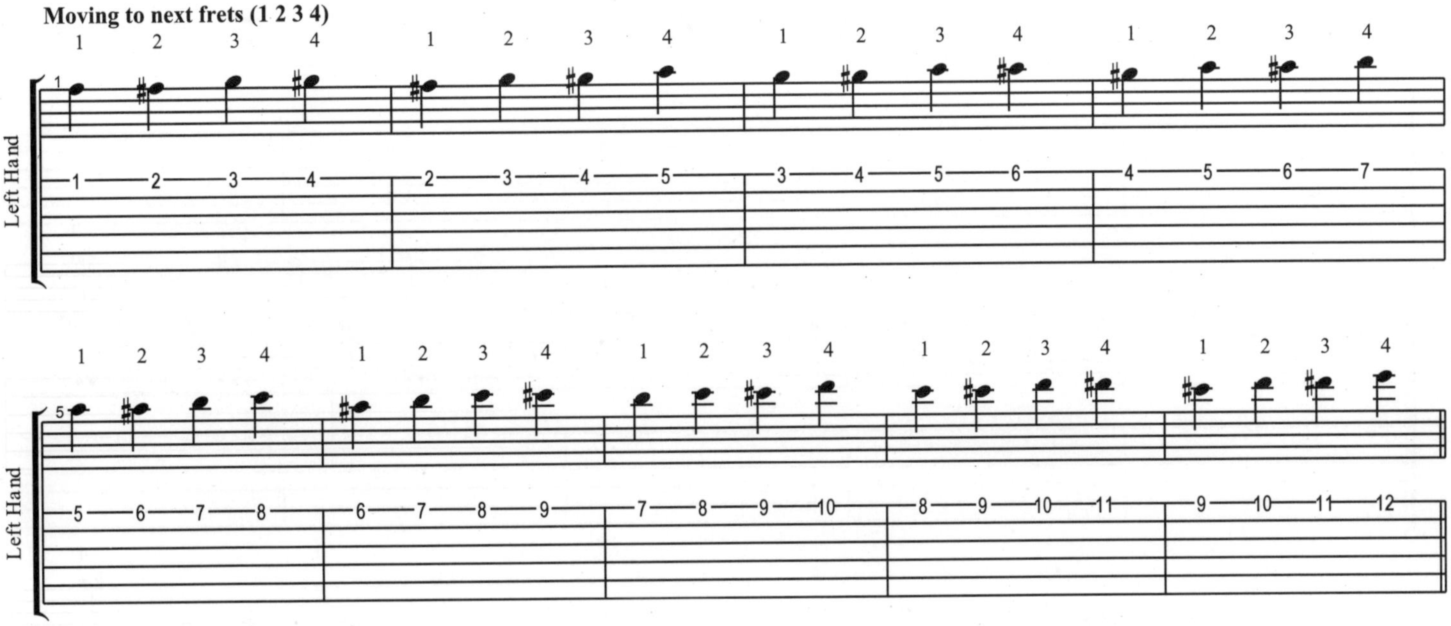

Going Back...

Improvisation - Ascending & Descending

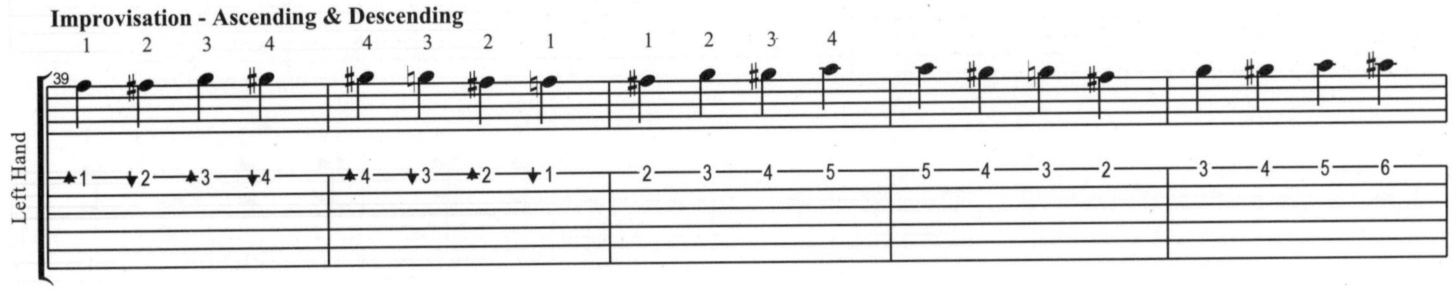

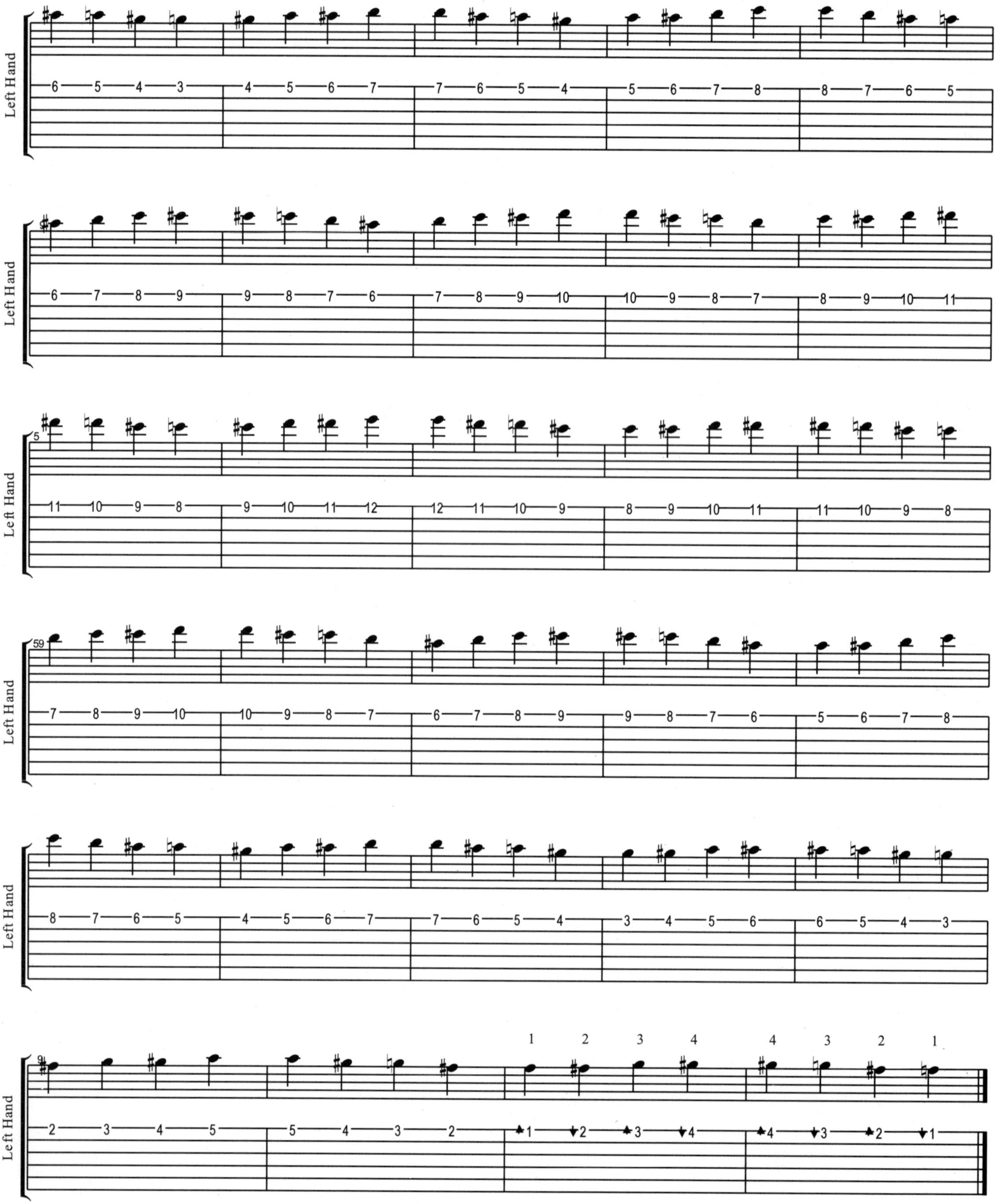
Left Hand
Left Hand
Left Hand
Left Hand
Left Hand
Left Hand
1 2 3 4 4 3 2 1

Exercise - 12

Left Hand Exercises

(Strength Building Exercises - 1)

Moving to Next Frets (1, 3, 2, 4)

Going Back...

Improvisation - Ascending & Descending

Left Hand
Going Back...

Exercise - 13

Left Hand Exercises

(Strength Building Exercises - 2)

Moving to Next Frets (1, 4, 3, 2)

Moving Back...

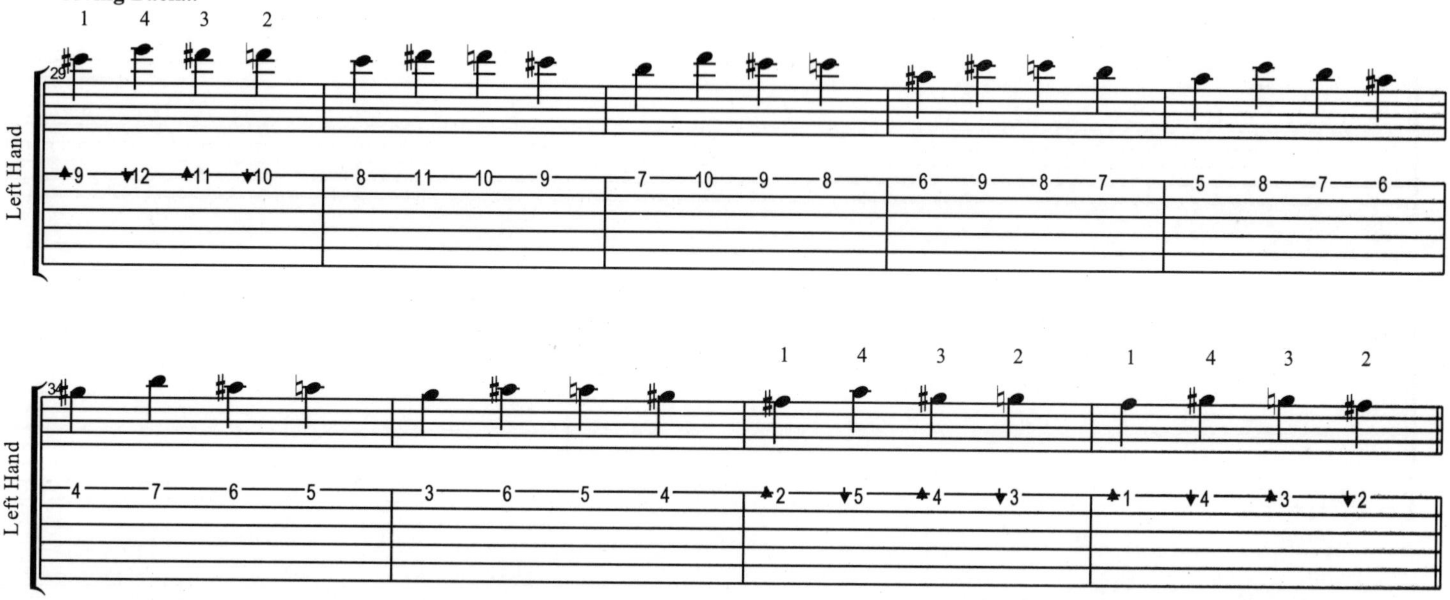

Improvisation - Ascending & Descending

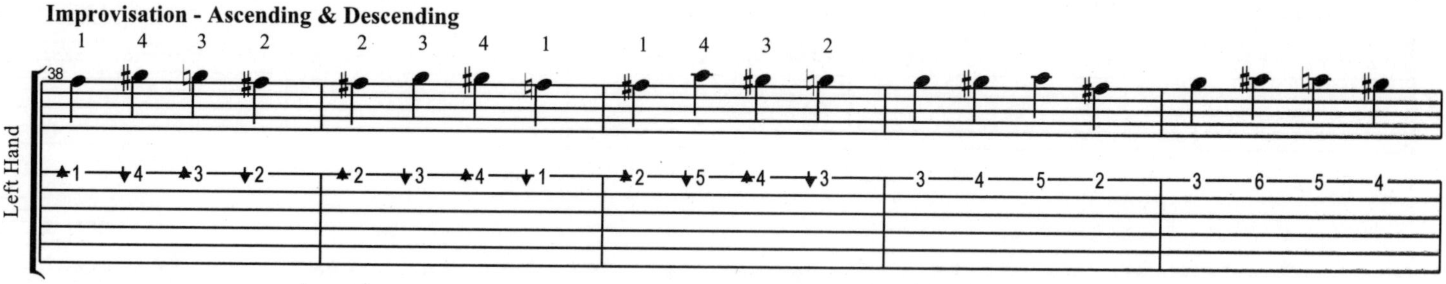

Left Hand
Going Back...

Exercise - 14

Left Hand Exercises

(Strength Building Exercises - 3)

Moderate ♩ = 180

Ascending & Descending

Left Hand
Left Hand
Left Hand
Left Hand
Left Hand
Left Hand

Exercise - 15

Left Hand Exercises

(Strength Building Exercises - 4)

Moderate ♩ = 180

Ascending & Descending

16
Left Hand
19
Left Hand
22
Left Hand
25
Left Hand
28
Left Hand
31
Left Hand

Exercise - 16

Left Hand Exercises

(Finger Control Exercises - 1)

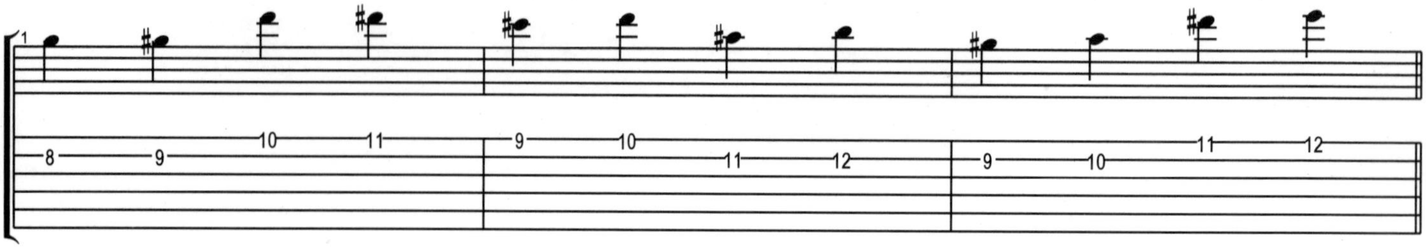

Going Back...

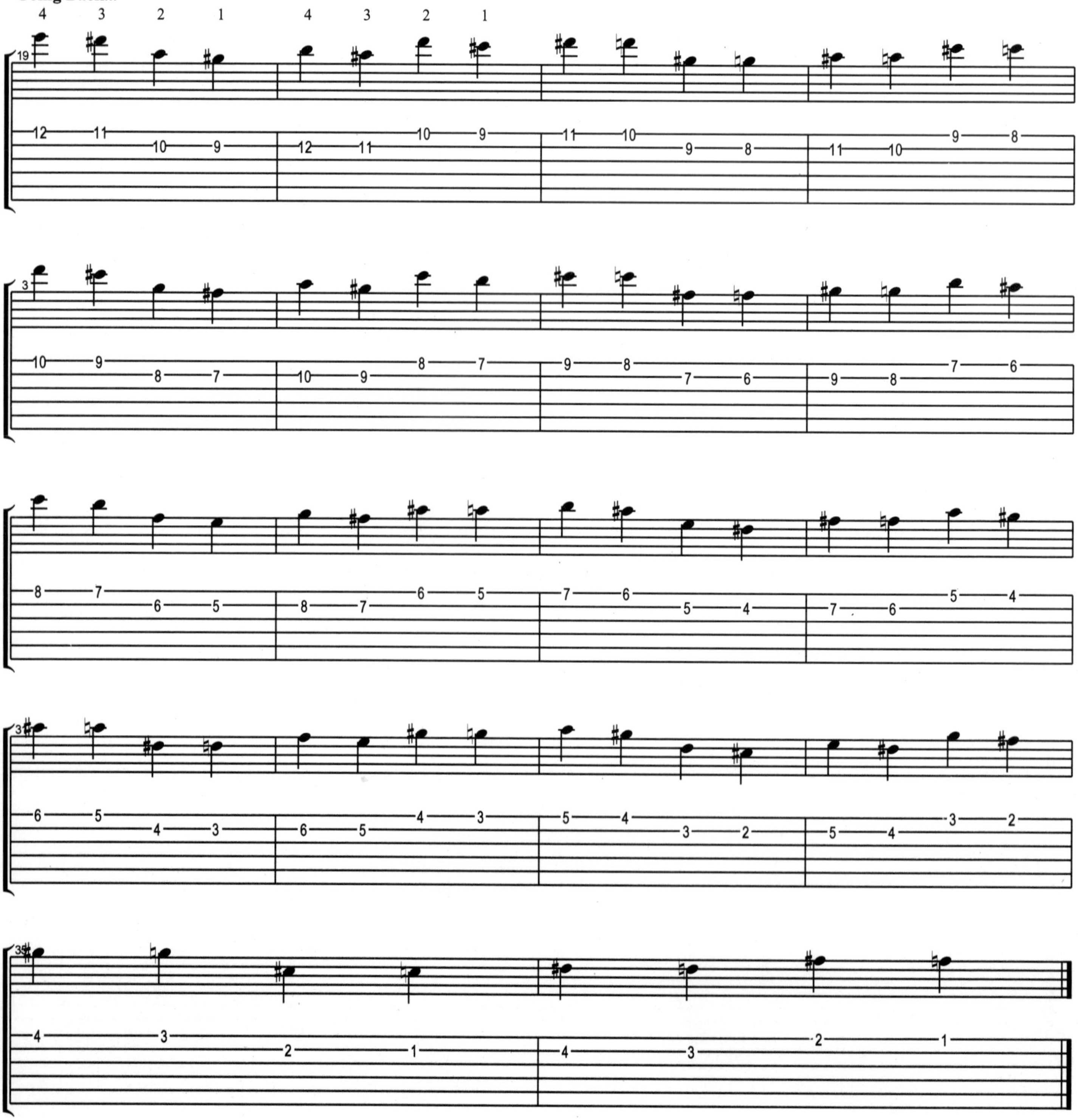

COMPOSITIONS

(A collection of special practice repertoire...)

Congratulations

Plectrum Guitar, Guitarmonk

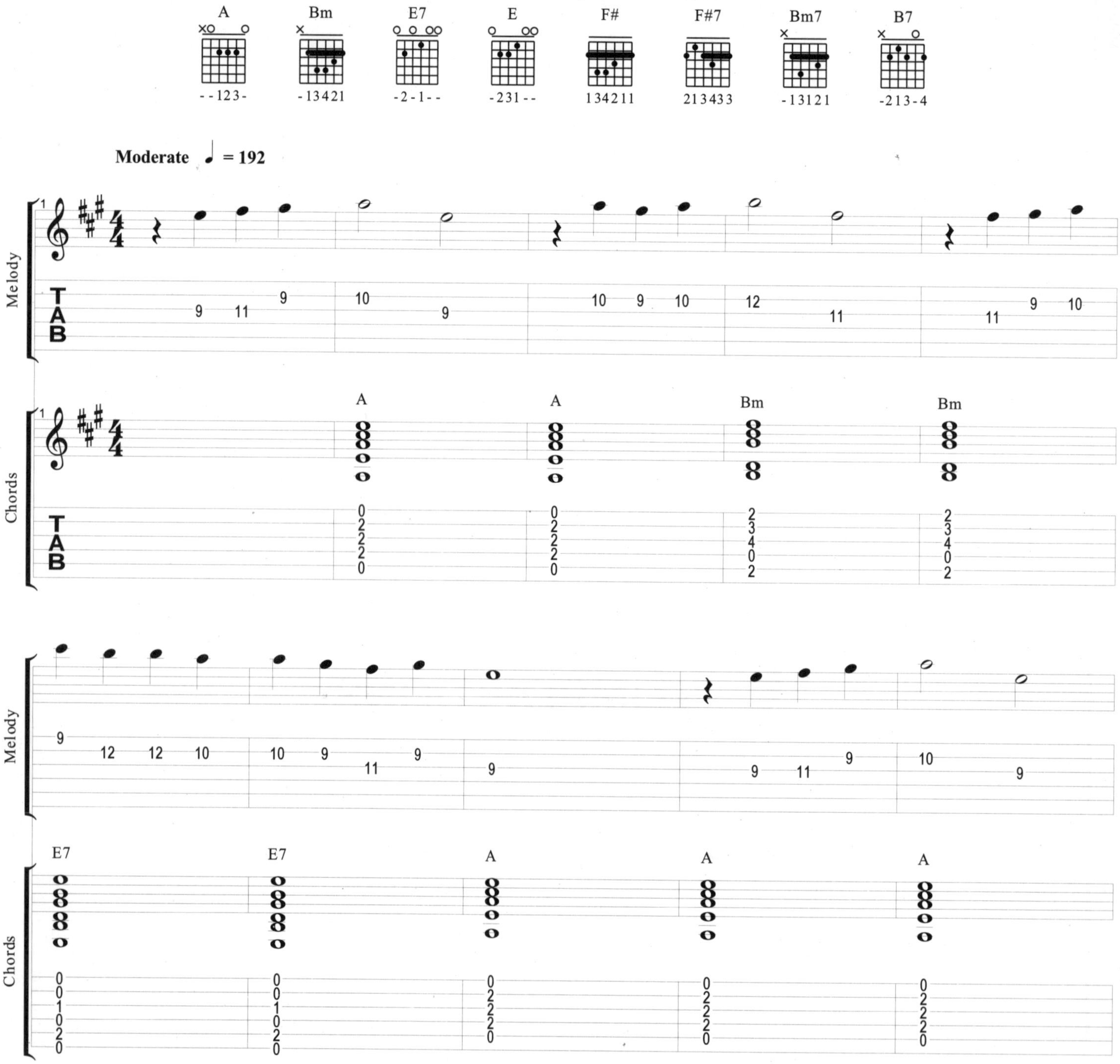

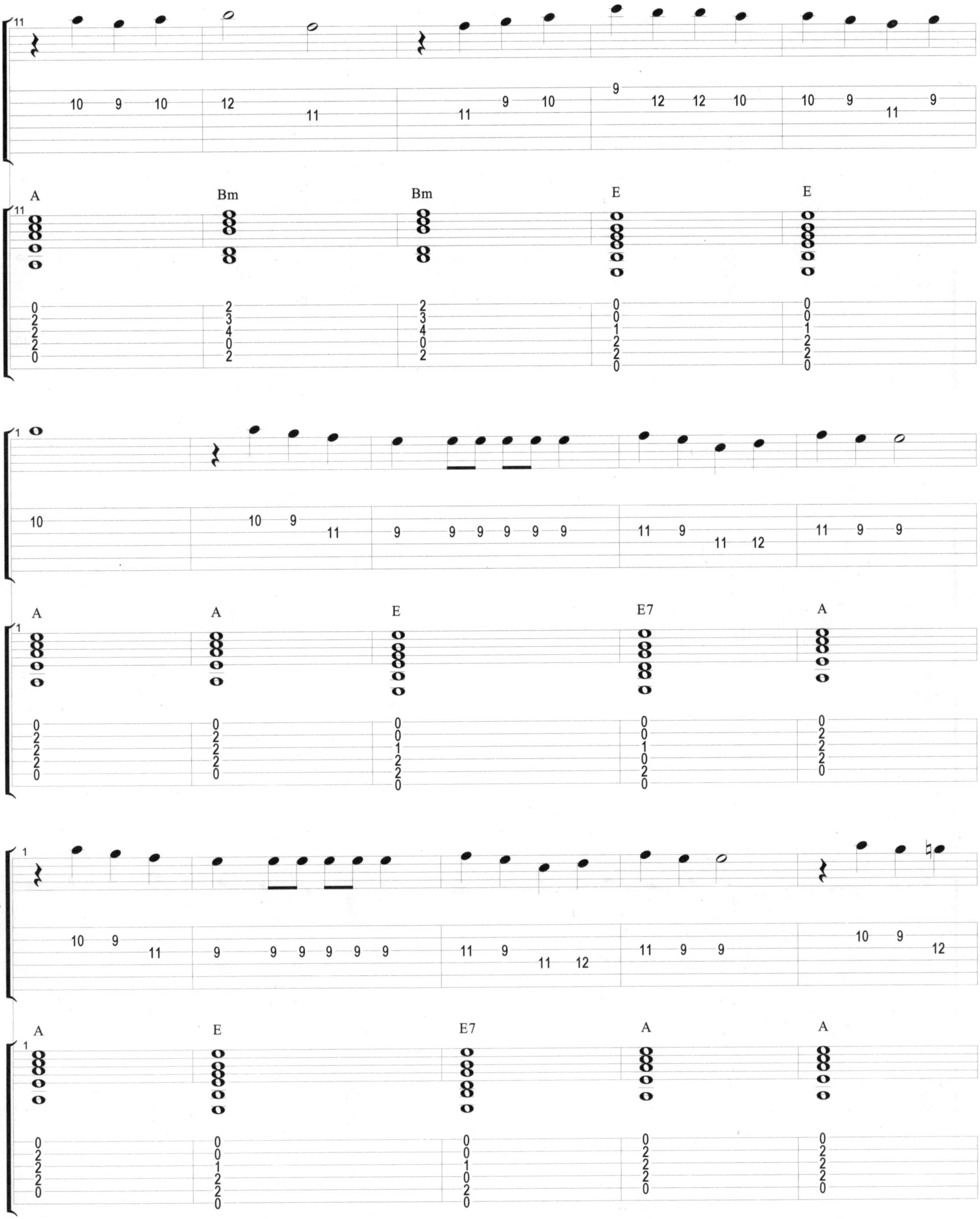
Melody
Chords
A
Bm
Bm
E
E
Melody
Chords
A
A
E
E7
A
Melody
Chords
A
E
E7
A
A

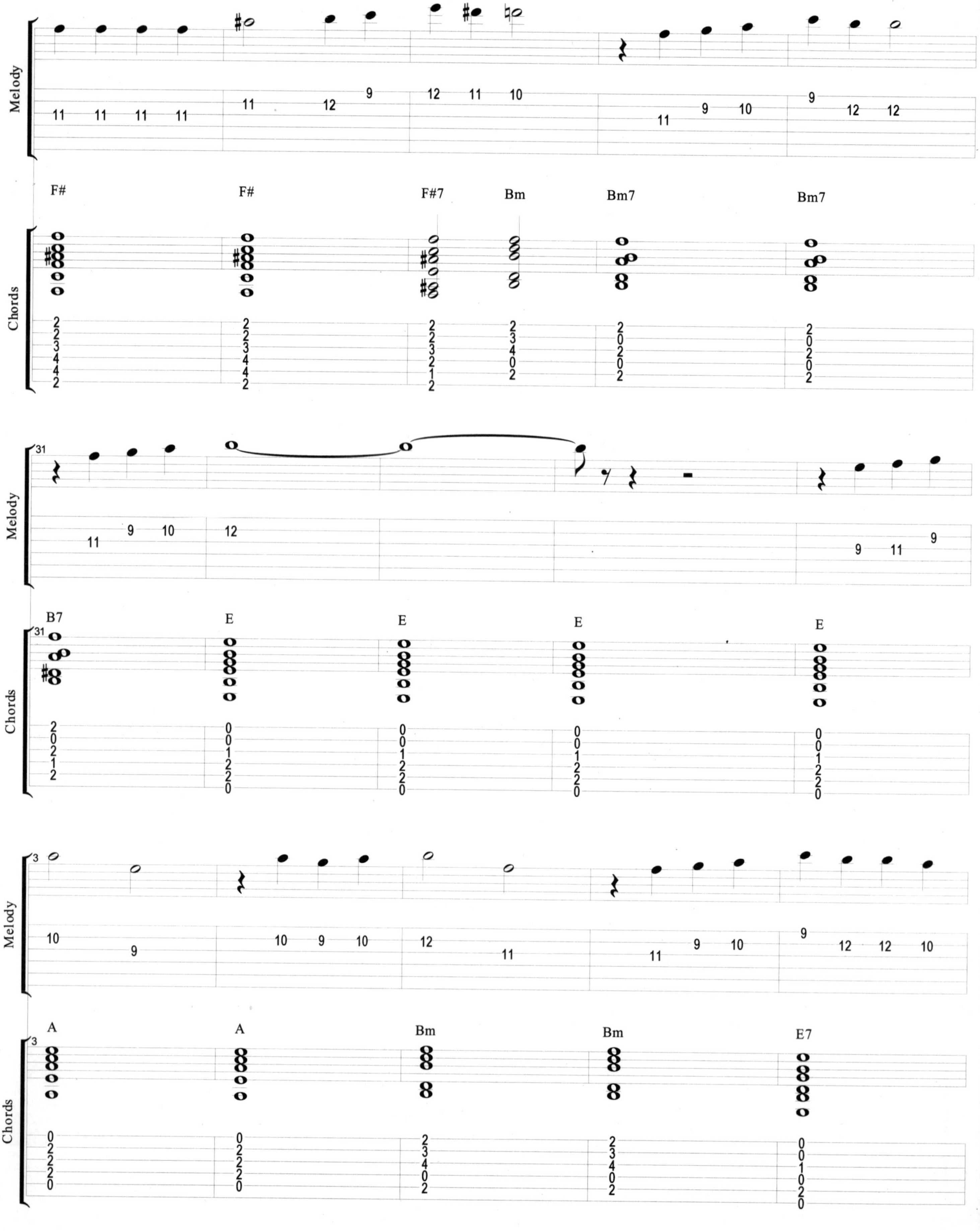
Melody
F#
F#
F#7
Bm
Bm7
Bm7
Chords
Melody
B7
E
E
E
E
Chords
Melody
A
A
Bm
Bm
E7
Chords

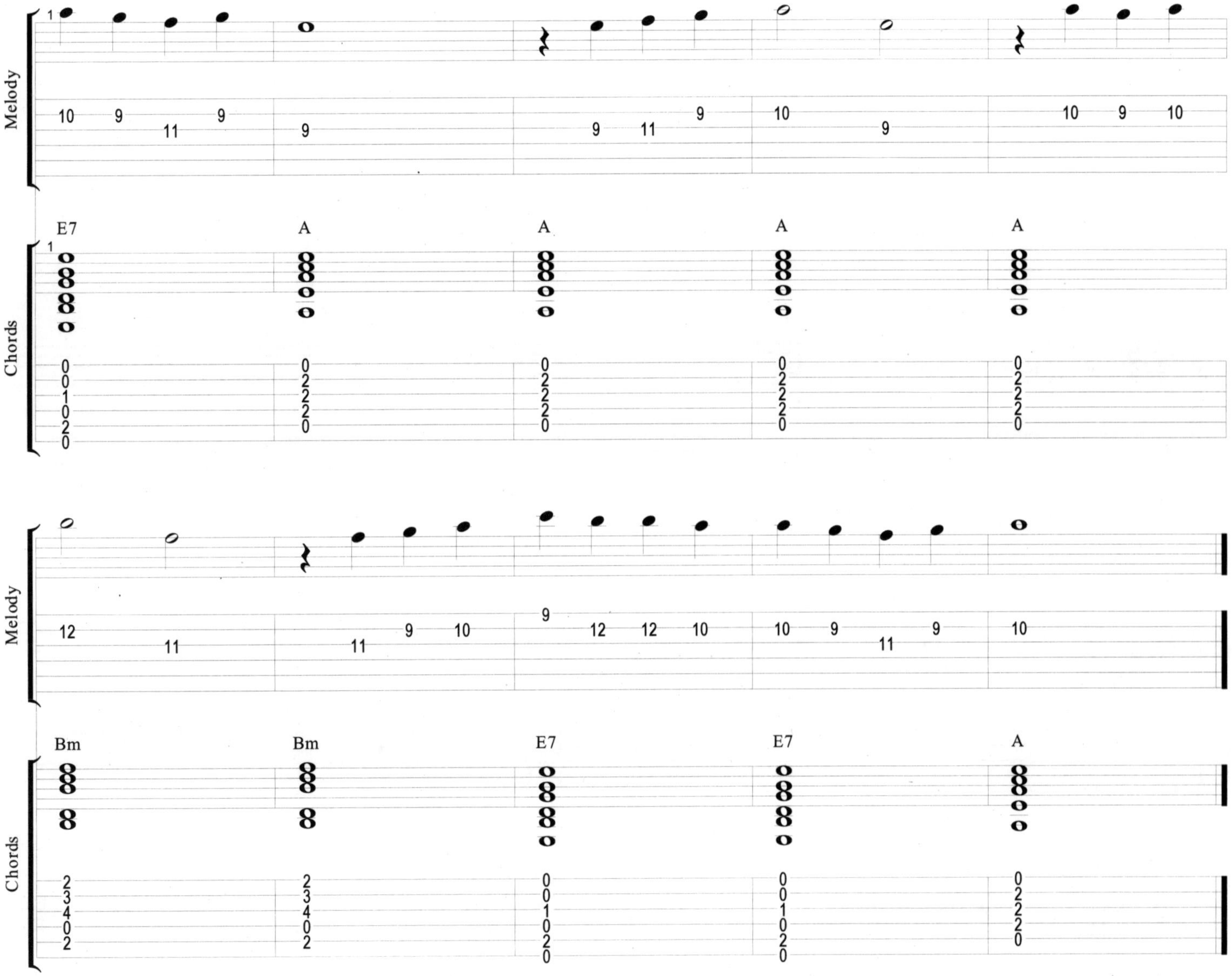
Melody
Chords
E7
A
A
A
A
Melody
Chords
Bm
Bm
E7
E7
A

Coventry Carol

Plectrum Guitar, Guitarmonk

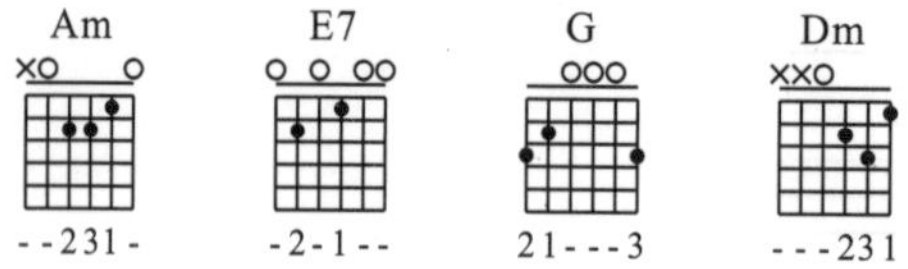

Melody
Chords
G
Am
G
Am
Dm
E7
Am
Dm
E7
Am
Am

Drowsy Maggie

Plectrum Guitar, Guitarmonk

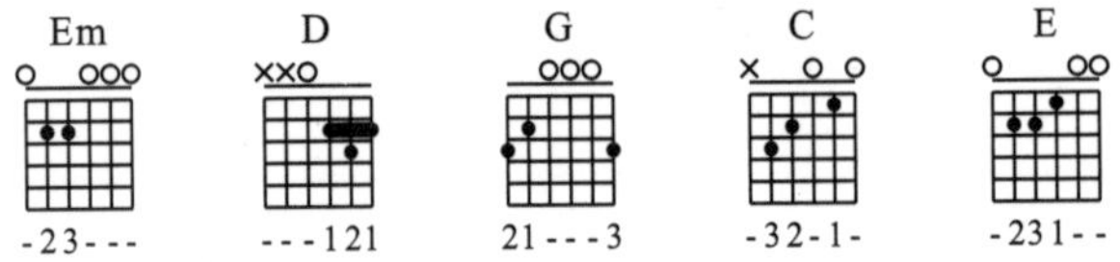

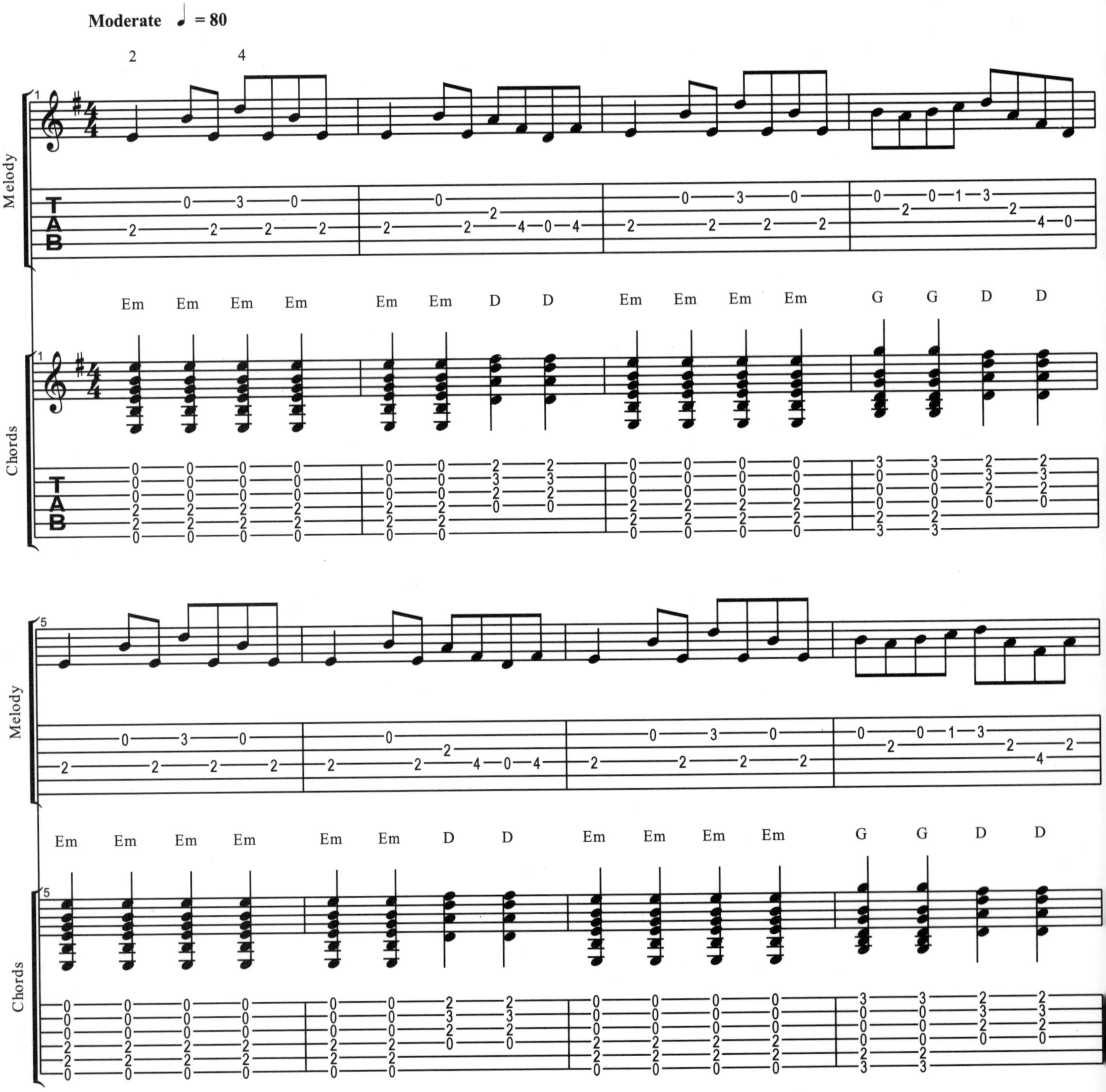

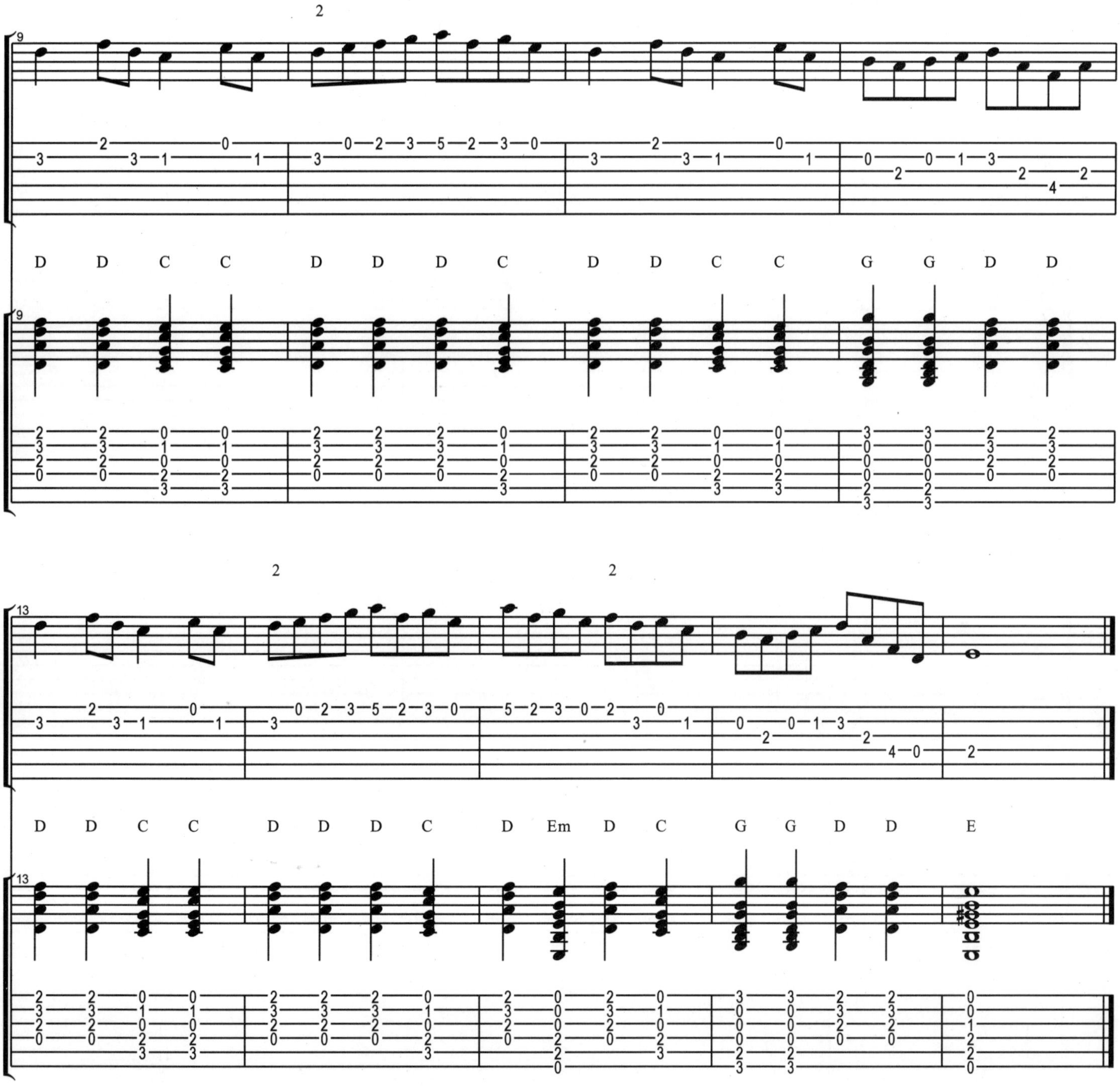
Melody
Chords
D D C C D D D C D D C C G G D D
D D C C D D D C D Em D C G G D D E

Greensleeves

Plectrum Guitar, Guitarmonk

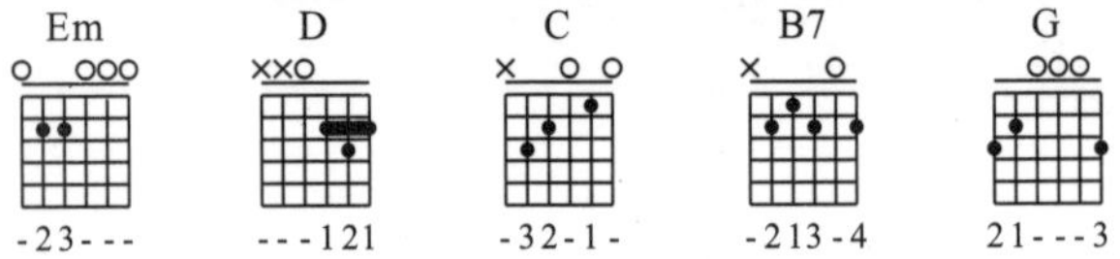

Melody
Chords
Em D D C B7
Melody
Chords
Em Em G G D
Melody
Chords
D Em Em B7 B7

Melody
Chords
G
G
D
D
Em
31
Melody
Chords
B7
Em
Em

Speak Softly Love

Plectrum Guitar, Guitarmonk

Godfather Theme by Andy Williams

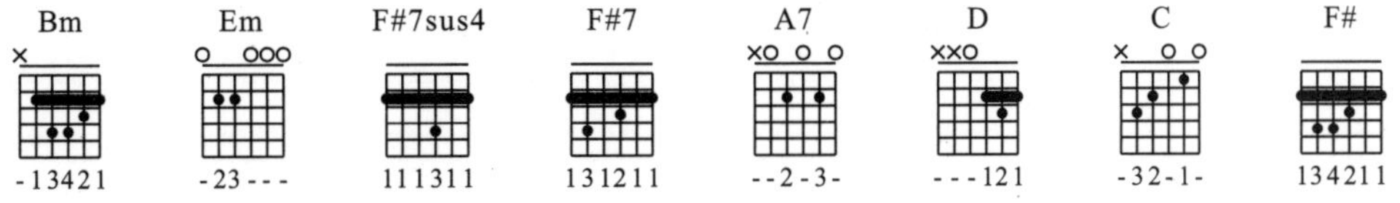

Moderately Slow ♩ = 100

Bridge

Melody
Chords
Bm F#7sus4 F#7 Bm Bm A7 A7 D D
C Em F# F# Bm Em Bm Bm
Bm Em Bm Em Em Em Em Bm Bm

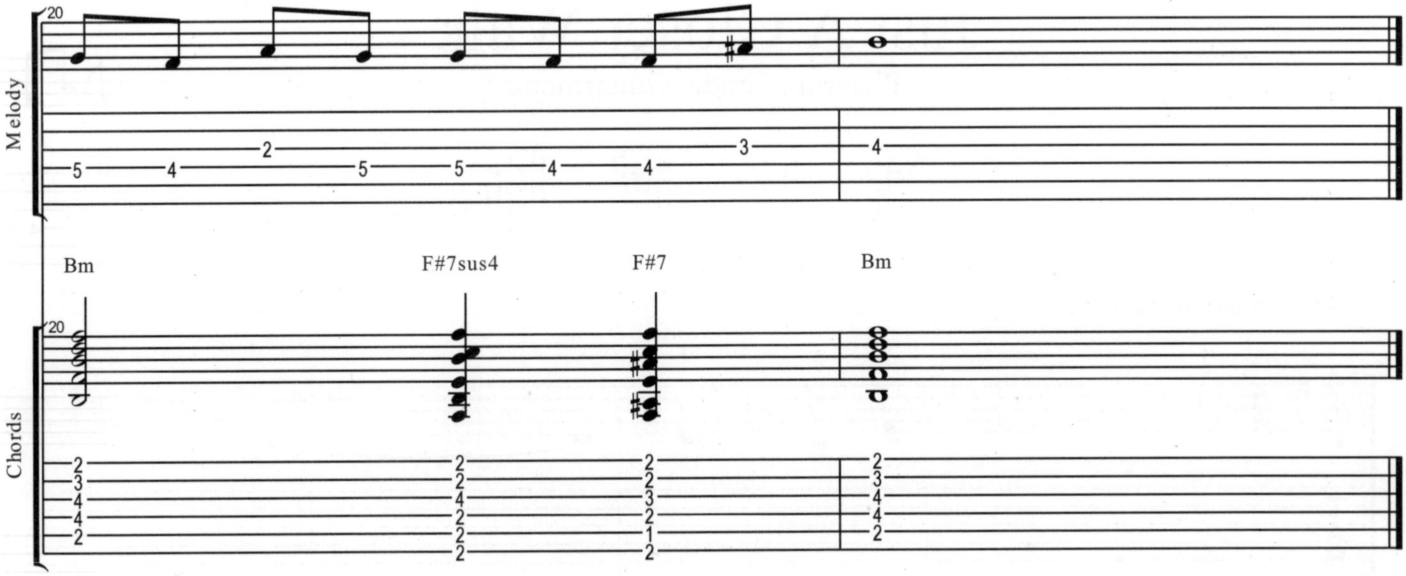
Melody
Bm
F#7sus4
F#7
Bm
Chords

Just A Closer Walk

Plectrum Grade, Guitarmonk

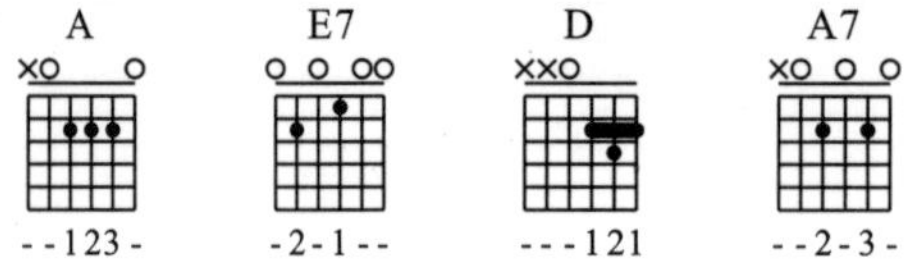

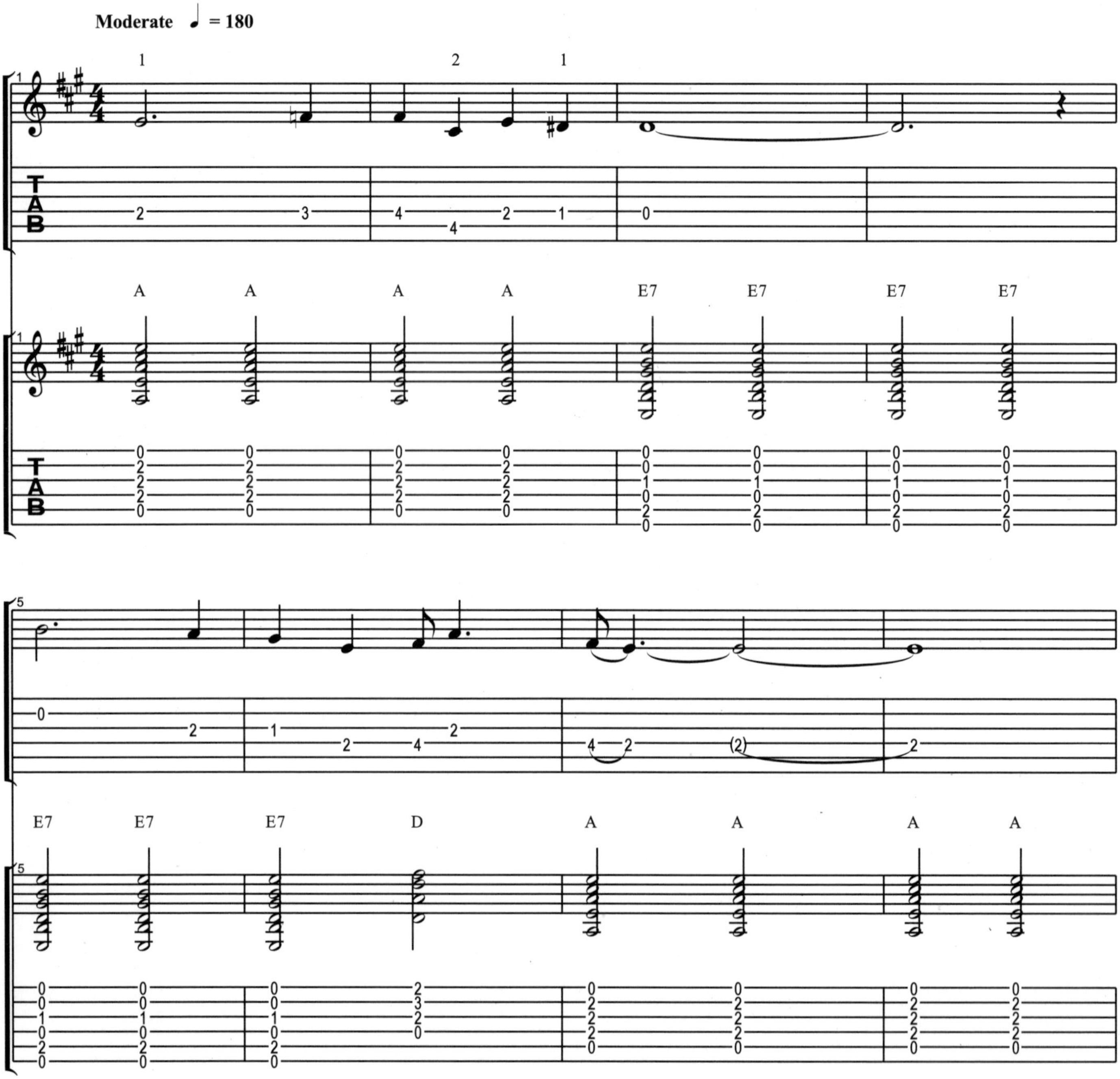

Melody
Chords
A A A7 A7 D D D D
4
Melody
Chords
A A E7 E7 A A A A

Nokia Theme

Plectrum Guitar, Guitarmonk

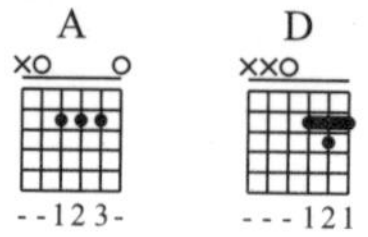

The God of Abraham Praise

Plectrum Guitar, Guitarmonk

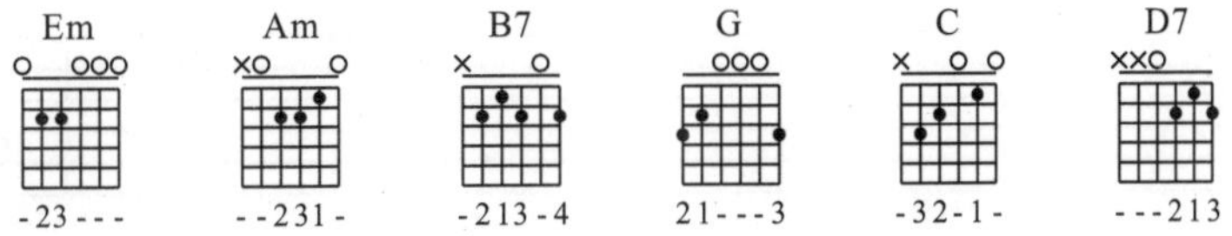

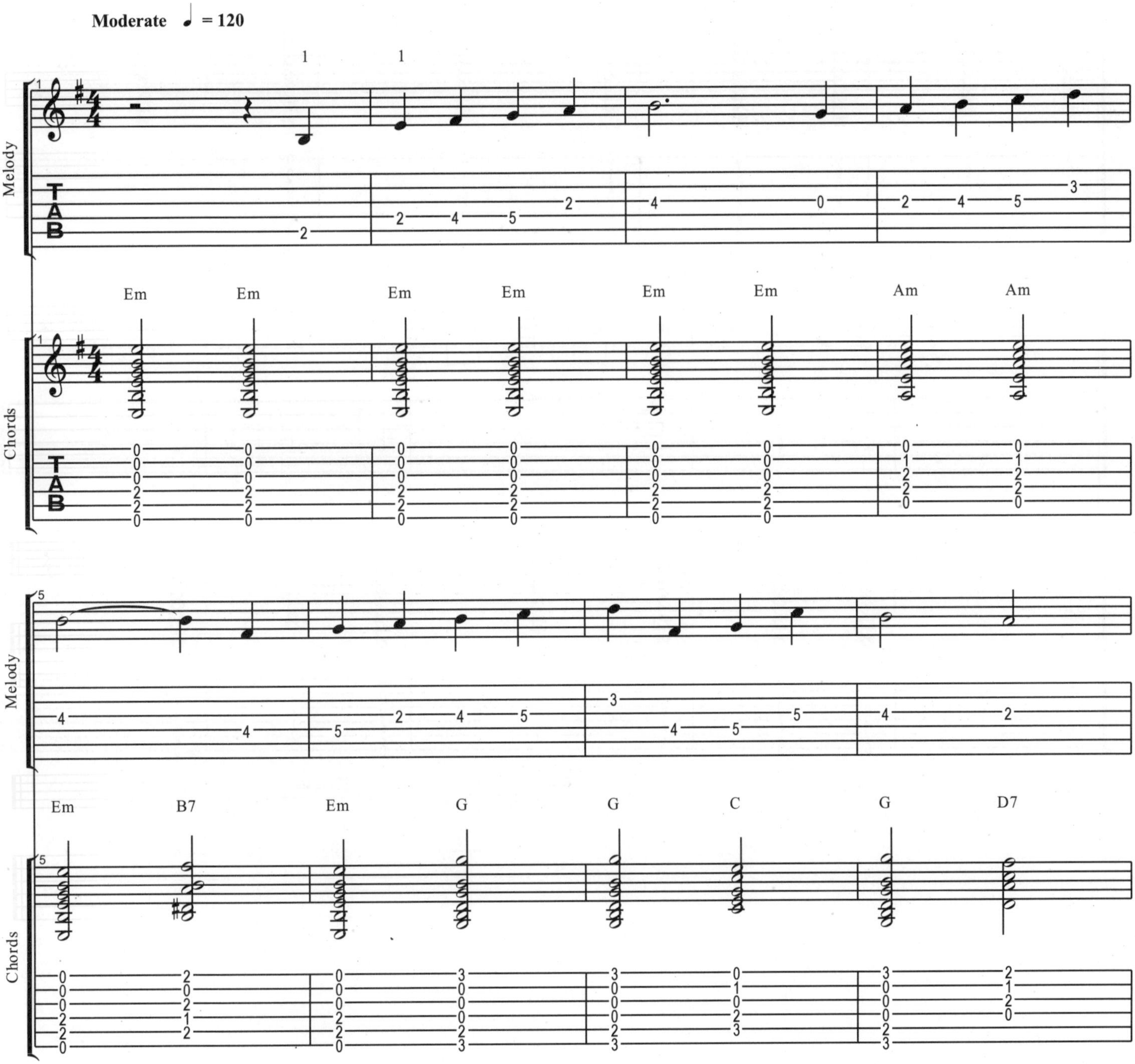

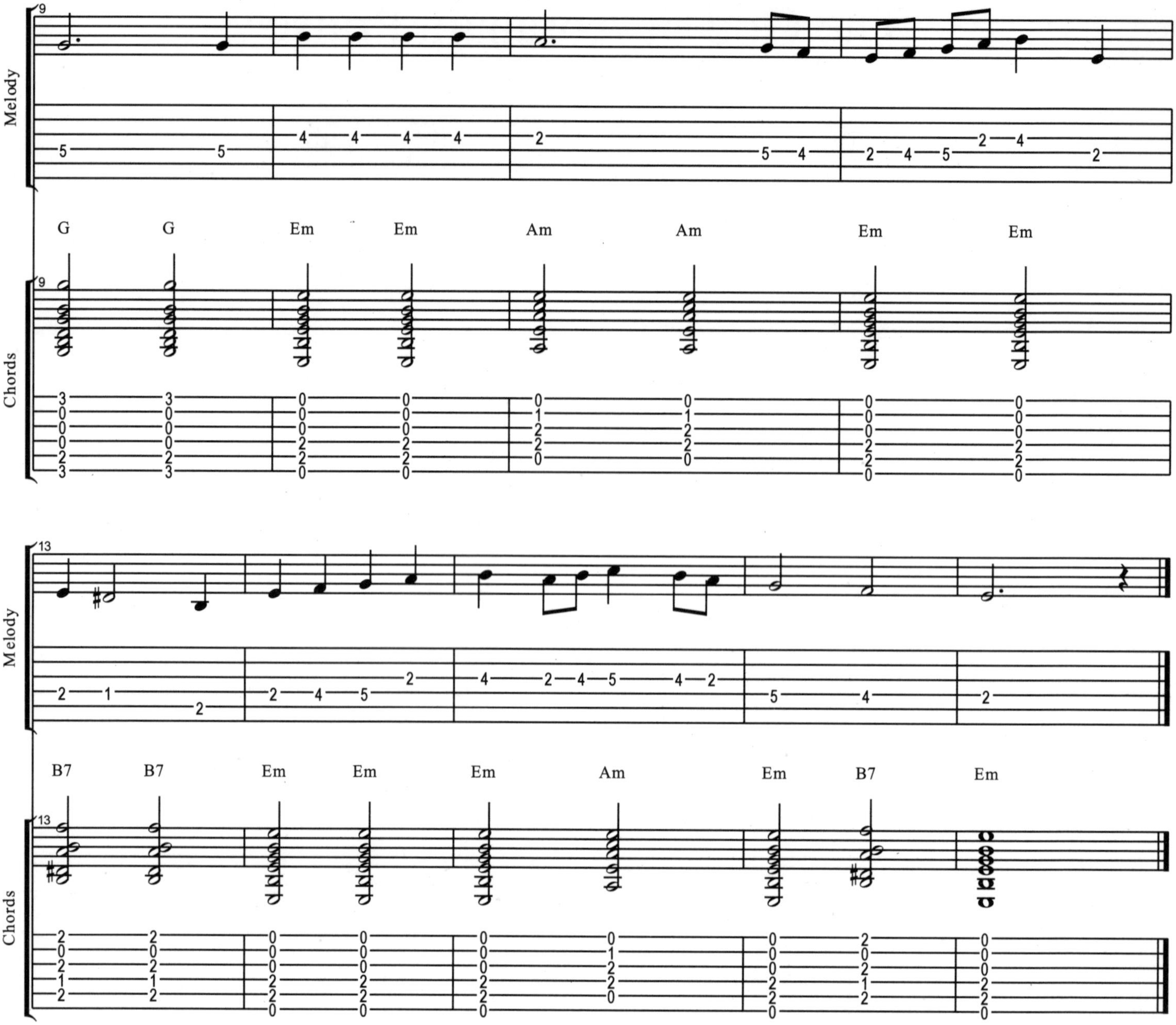
Melody
Chords
G G Em Em Am Am Em Em
B7 B7 Em Em Em Am Em B7 Em

This Train

Plectrum Guitar, Guitarmonk

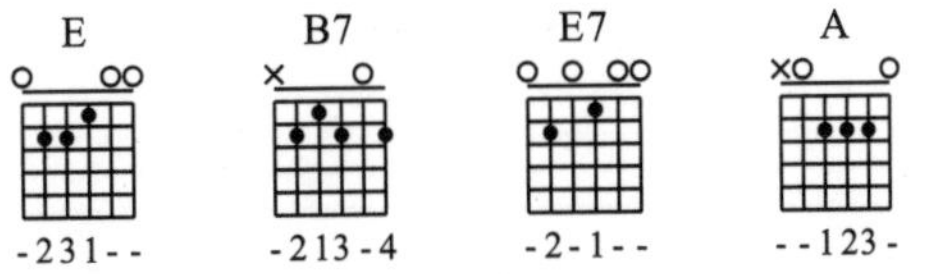

Moderate ♩ = 180

Melody
Chords
E E E7 E7 A A A A
Melody
Chords
E E A A E E E E

When the saints go marching in

Plectrum Guitar, Guitarmonk

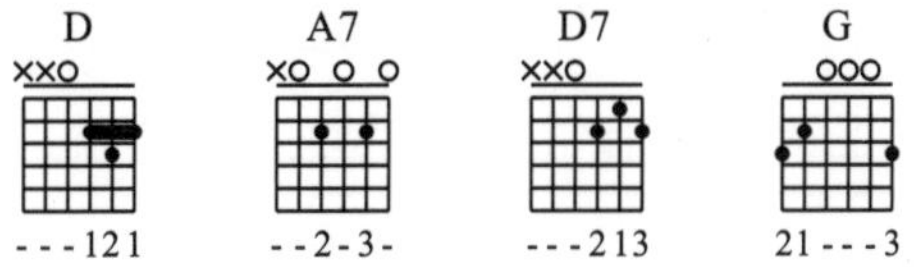

Melody
Chords
A7 A7 D D D7 D7 G G
Melody
Chords
G G D D D A7 D G D

INDIAN Pop Songs

MUSIC CHORDS AND LYRICS

(A beautiful repertoire for all music lovers and students...)

INDIAN SONGS

1. Ajeeb Dastan hai Yeh
2. Chura Liya
3. Pya Dewana Hota hai
4. Tumse hi
5. Maa
6. Rimjhim Gire Sawan
7. Pehla Pehla Pyar hai
8. Pehla Nasha

AJEEB DASTAN HAI YE

1

Artist: Lata Mangeshkar
Album: Dil Apna Aur Preet Parai
Scale: D Major

```
D                                                Em        A
(Ajeeb daastan hain ye, kahan shuru kahan khatam,
                          G                          D
Ye manzilen hain kaunsi, na wo samajh sake na hum)        X 2

                          G                        D
(Ye roshni ke saath kyun, dhuaan utha chiraag se)         X 2
A                          G                             D
Ye khwaab dekhti hoon main, ke jag padi hoon khwaab se,

D                                                Em        A
(Ajeeb daastan hain ye, kahan shuru kahan khatam,
                          G                          D
Ye manzilen hain kaunsi, na wo samajh sake na hum)

                   G                      D
(Kisi ka pyar leke tum, naya jahan basaoge)               X 2
A                 G                      D
Ye shaam jab bhi aayegi, tum humko yaad aaoge

D                                                Em        A
(Ajeeb daastan hain ye, kahan shuru kahan khatam,
                          G                          D
Ye manzilen hain kaunsi, na wo samajh sake na hum)

                          G                    D
(Mubarke tumhen ke tum, kisi ke noor ho gaye)             x 2
A                  G                   D
Kisi ke itne paas ho, ke sabse door ho gaye

D                                                Em        A
(Ajeeb daastan hain ye, kahan shuru kahan khatam,
                          G                          D
Ye manzilen hain kaunsi, na wo samajh sake na hum)
```

Ajeeb Dastan hai ye...

Kahan Shuru kahan Khatam,

Ye Manzile hai kaunsi...

Na wo Samajh Sake Na hum,

Ye Roshni ke Sath kyun,

Dhuaan Utha Chirag se...

Ye Khwaab Dekhti hoon mai,

Ke jag padi hoo khawab se...

Kisi ka pyar leke tum,

Naya Jahan Basonge,

Ye shaam jab bhi aayegi,

Tum humko yaad aaoge,

Ajeeb Dastan hai ye...

CHURA LIYA

Artist: Mohd. Rafi, Asha Bhonsle
Album: Yaadon ki Baraat
Scale: A minor

```
        Am                              G
(Chura liya hain tumne jo dil ko,
Am                          E
Nazar nahin churana sanam,
Am                           G      Am                   E
Badal ke meri tum zindagani, kahin badal na jana sanam)
A4       Am  E           Am   G        A Major
     Le liya   dil, ho hai mera dil, hai dil lekar mujhko na  behlana,

Am              CM7
Chura liya!
```

(Chura liya hai tumne ....kahin badal na jana Sanam)

```
Am                G                C
(Bahaar ban ke aaoon, kabhi tumhari duniya mein,
Am             Dm              Am
Guzar Na jaaye ye din kabhi, isi tamanna mein)              x 2
A4                G              Am   G
          Tum mere ho, ho tum mere ho
         A
Aaj tum itna wada karte jana,

 Am             G
Chura liya!
```

(Chura liya hai tumne ....kahin badal na jana Sanam)

Chura Liya hai tumne jo

Dil ko...,

Nazar nahi churana Sanam,

Badal ke mere tum zindagani,

Kahi badal na jana Sanam,

Le liya dil, ho mera dil,

Hai dil lekar, mujhko,

Na behlana,

Chura liya...

```
        Am               G                  C
        Sazaaoonga ka lutkar bhi, tere bada ki daali ko
        Am               Dm              Am
        Lahoon zigar ka doonga, haseen labon ki laali Ko
A4               G        Am G      A                                    Am      CM7
        Hain wafa kya, is jahan ko, ek din dikh la doonga main dewana, Chura liya!
```

(Chura liya hai tumne ....kahin badal na jana Sanam)

PYAR DEEWANA HOTA HAI

3

Artist: Kishore Kumar
Album: Kati Patang
Scale: F Major

```
 F                Eb
(Pyar dewana hota hain,
    F      Eb    F
Mas tana hota hain,
F                   Eb
Har khushi se, har gam se,
   F      Eb     F
Be gana hota hain)                   X 2

F                    F
(Shama kahe parwane se,
                 Bb
Pare chala ja,
Eb               F
Meri tarah jal jayega,
Eb               F
Yahan nahi aa)                       X 2

F         Eb              F    Eb    F
Wo nahin sunta usko, dhal jana hota hain,
F              Eb           F      Eb  F
Har khushi se, har gam se, be gana hota hain,


(Pyar dewana hota hain....begana hota hai)


F                    F
(Rahen koi sau pardon mein,
                  Bb
Dare sharam se,
Eb                F
Nazar aji lakh churaye,
Eb                 F
Koi sanam se)           X 2

F         Eb              F     Eb    F
Aa hi jata hain jispe dil, aa na hota hain,
F              Eb           F     Eb   F
har khushi se, har gam se, be gana hota hain,
```

Pyar Dewana hota hai,

Mastana hota hai,

Har Khushi se,

Har gam se,

Begaana hota hai,

Shama kahe Parwane Se,

Pare Chala Ja,

Meri Tarah Jal Jayega,

Yaha Nahi aa...

```
F               Eb
(Pyar dewana hota hain,
    F      Eb    F
Mas tana hota hain,
F                   Eb
Har khushi se, har gam se,
   F      Eb     F
Be gana hota hain)
```

TUMSE HI

Artist: Mohit Chauhan
Album: Jab We Met
Scale: F# Major

F# C# B
Na hai yeh pana,
B C# F#
Na khona hi hai,
F# C# B
Tera na hona, jaane,
B C# F#
Kuyn hona hi hai,
C# B
Tum Se hi din hota hai,
C# B
Surmayi shaam aati hai,
F#
Tum Se hi tum se hi,
C# B
Har ghadi saans aati hai,
C# B
Zindagi kehlati hai,
F#
Tum Se hi tum se hi,
F# C# B
Na hai yeh pana,
B C# B
Na khona hi hai,
F# C# B
Tera na hona, jaane,
B C# F#
Kuyn hona hi hai,

F# A#m
Aankho mein aankhe teri,
B
Bahoo mein bahe teri,
A#m B C#
Mera na mujh mein kuch raha,
B
Hua kya,
F# A#m
Baton mein batein teri,
B
Rathe saogathe meri,
A#m B C#
Kyun tera sab yeh ho gaya,
B
Hua kya,
C# B
Mein kahin bhi jaata hun,
C# B
Tum Se hi mil jaata hun,
F#
Tum se hi tum se hi,
C# B
Shor mein khamoshi hai,
C# B
Thodi si behoshi hai,
F#
Tum se hi tum se hi,

Na hai ye pana..
Na khona hi hai,
Tera na hona, jaane..
Kyu hona hi hai,
Tumse hi din hota hai
Surmayi shaam aati hai,
Tum se hi, tum se hi,

F# A#m
Aadha sa vaada kabhi,
B
Aadhe se zyada kabhi,
A#m B C#
Jee chahe karlu is tarah,
B
Wafa ka,
F# A#m
Chode na chute kabhi,
B
Tode na toote kabhi,
A#m B C# B
Jo daaga tum se jud gaya, Wafa ka,

C# B
Mein tera sarmaya hun,
C# B
Jo bhi mein ban paya hun,
F#
Tum se hi tum se hi,
C# B
Raaste mil jate hai,
C# B
Manzile mil jati hai,
F#
Tum se hi tum se hi,

F# C# B
Na hai yeh pana,
B C# F#
Na khona he hai,
F# C# B
Tera na hona, jaane,
B C# B
Kyun hona he hai,

MAA

Artist: Shankar Mahadevan
Album: Tare Zameen Par
Scale: C Major

C F C
Main kabhi... batlata nahin,
G F C
Par andhere se dartaa hoon main maa,
C F C
Yu to main... dikhlata nahin,
G F C
Teri parwah karta hoon main maa...,
F G C
Tujhe sab hai pata... hai na maa,
F G C
Tujhe sab hai pata......aa meri maa,

C F C
Bheed mein... yu na chodo mujhe,
G F C
Ghar laut ke bhi aana paaon maa,
C F C
Bhejna... itna door mujhko tu,
G F C
Yaad bhi tujhko aana paaoon maa,
F G C
Kya itna bura hoon main maa,
F G C
Kya itna bura....aa.. hoon main maa,

Main Kabhi...,

Batlata nahi...,

Par andhere se darta hoo main ma...,

Yu to main, dikhlatanahi,

Teri parwah karta hoon main maa..,

Tujhe sab hai pata...,

Hai na maa..,

C E7
Jab bhi kabhi...papa mujhe,
Am G# Fm7/Fm C
Jo zor se... jhoola jhulate hain maa...,
C E7
Meri nazar... dhoonde tujhe,
Am G# Fm7/Fm C
Sochu yahin... tu aake thamegi maa...,

C F C
Tumse main... ye kehta nahi,
G F C
Par main sehem jata hoon maa,
C F C
Chehre pe... aane deta nahi,
G F C
Dil hi dil mein ghabrata hoon maa,

F G C
Tujhe sab hai pata hai na maa,
F G C
Tujhe sab hai pata... ... ...meri maa ,

RIMJHIM GIRE SAWAN

6

Artist: Kishore Kumar
Album: Manzil
Scale: D minor

Hmmmmmm...

Dm
Rimjhim gire sawan,
Gm
Sulag sulag jaaye mann,
C
Bheege aaj is mausam mein,
Am Dm A Dm
Lagi kaisi yeh agan,
Dm
Rimjhim gire sawan,

A Gm A
Jab ghunghroon si bajti hain boondein,
A7 Gm Dm
Armaan hamare palken na moondein, **X 2**
Dm Gm
Kaise dekhen sapne nayan, sulag sulag jaaye mann,
C
Bheege aaj is mausam mein,
Am Dm A Dm
Lagi kaisi yeh agan,
Dm
Rimjhim gire sawan,

Rimjhim gire sawan,

Sulag sulag jaaye mann,

Bheege aaj is mausam mein,

Lagi kaisi yeh agan,

Rimjhim gire sawan....

A Gm A
Mehfil mein kaise, kehden kisise,
A7 Gm Dm
Dil bandh raha hai kis ajnabi se,
Dm Gm
Haaye karen ab kya jatan,

Sulag sulag jaaye mann,
C
Bheege aaj is mausam mein,
Am Dm A Dm
Lagi kaisi yeh agan,

Dm
Rimjhim gire sawan,
Gm
Sulag sulag jaaye mann,
C
Bheege aaj is mausam mein,
Am Dm A Dm
Lagi kaisi yeh agan,
Dm
Rimjhim gire sawan,

PEHLA PEHLA PYAR HAI

7

Artist: S.P. Balasubramaniam
Album: Hum Aapke hain kaun
Scale: D minor

Dm A
Pehla pehla pyar hai,
A7 Dm
Pehli pehli baar hai ,
D C7
Jaan ke bhi anjaana ,
Gm F Dm|C |Bb |A7
Kaisa mera yaar hai..,

Dm A
Pehla pehla pyar hai ...,

Dm
Uski nazar,
G Dm F
Palkon ki chilman se mujhe dekhti, uski nazar,
Dm
Uski haya,
G Dm F
Apni hi chaahat ka raaz kholti, uski haya,
D C7
Chhup ke kare jo wafa,
Gm F Dm|C |Bb |A7
Aisa mera yaar hai,

Dm A
Pehla pehla pyar hai ...,

Pehla pehla pyar hai,

Pehli pehli baar hai,

Jaan ke bhi anjaana,

Kaisa mera yaar hai..,

Pehla pehla pyar hai...,

Dm
Wo hai nisha,
G Dm F
Wo hi meri zindagi ki bhor hai, wo hai nisha,
Dm
Use hai pata,
G Dm F
Uske hi haathon mein meri dor hai, use hai pata,
D C7
Saare jahan se juda,
Gm F Dm|C |Bb |A7
Aisa mera pyaar hai,

Dm A
Pehla pehla pyar hai,
A7 Dm
Pehli pehli baar hai,
D C7
Jaan ke bhi anjaana,
Gm F Dm|C |Bb |A7
Kaisa mera yaar hai..,

PEHLE NASHA

8

Artist: Udit Narayan & Sadhna sargam
Album: Jo Jeeta Wohi Sikander
Scale: F Major

F **C**
Pehla nasha, pehla khumaar,
F **Gm** **C**
Naya pyaar hain , naya intzaar,
Dm **F** **Dm** **C**
Karloo main kya apna haal, ae dile beqaraar,
Dm **F** **C**
Mere dile beqarar, tu hi bata..

F **Bb** **Gm** **F**
Udta hi phiru, In hawaaon mein kahin,
Bb **C** **F**
Ya main jhool jaun, in ghataaon mein kahin,) **X 2**
Cm **F**
Ik kardoon aasmaan aur zameen,
Bb **Gm** **Bb/C/F**
Kaho yaaro kya karoon, kya nahin..

F **C**
Pehla nasha, pehla khumaar,

F **Bb** **Gm** **F**
Usne baat ki, kuch aise dhang se,
Bb **C** **F**
Sapne, de gaya, wo hazaaron rang ke,
Cm **F**
Reh jaaun jaise main haar ke,
Bb **Gm** **Bb/C/F**

Aur chume who mujhe pyaar se

F **C**
Pehla nasha, pehla khumaar,

Pehla Nasha, Pehla Khumaar,

Naya Pyaar hain, naya Intzaar

Karloo main kya apna haal

Ae dile beqaraar,

Mere dile beqaraar,

Tu hi Bata...